Vegetables

Nancy Dickmann

Heinemann
LIBRARY

Chicago, Illinois

www.capstonepub.com
Visit our website to find out
more information about
Heinemann-Raintree books.

To order:

☎ Phone 888-454-2279

🖥 Visit www.capstonepub.com
to browse our catalog and order online.

©2012 Heinemann Library
an imprint of Capstone Global Library, LLC
Chicago, Illinois

Edited by Rebecca Rissman and Adrian Vigliano
Designed by Joanna Hinton-Malivoire
Picture research by Elizabeth Alexander
Production by Victoria Fitzgerald
Originated by Capstone Global Library Ltd
Printed in the United States of America by Worzalla Publishing.

15 14 13 12 11
10 9 8 7 6 5 4 3 2 1

Library of Congress Cataloging-in-Publication Data
Cataloging-in-Publication data is on file at the Library of Congress.

ISBN 978-1-4329-6974-5 (hc) -- ISBN 978-1-4329-6981-3 (pb)

Acknowledgments
We would like to thank the following for permission to reproduce
photographs: © Capstone Publishers pp.16, 22 (Karon Dubke); Alamy
pp.20, 23 middle (© MBI); Corbis pp.10 (© amanaimages), 21 (© Gideon
Mendel); Getty Images p.17 (Robert Daly/OJO Images); iStockphoto
pp.4, 23 bottom (© Dana Bartekoske), 7 (© David T. Gomez), 8 (© Shane
Cummins), 11 (© Jon Faulknor), 14 (© Doug Schneider), 15 (© Francisco
Romero), 23 top (© Mark Hatfield); Photolibrary pp.5 (Image Source),
6 (Mode Images), 12 (OJO Images/Andrew Olney), 13 (Jasper James);
Shutterstock pp.9 (© Elena Kalistratova), 18 (© Monkey Business Images);
U.S. Department of Agriculture, Center for Nutrition Policy and Promotion
p.19.

Front cover photograph of a variety of vegetables reproduced with
permission of Corbis (© Ed Young/AgStock Images). Back cover photograph
of a girl eating a carrot reproduced with permission of iStockphoto (© Doug
Schneider).

Every effort has been made to contact copyright holders of material
reproduced in this book. Any omissions will be rectified in subsequent
printings if notice is given to the publishers.

Contents

What Are Vegetables?

A vegetable is a type of plant
we eat.

Eating vegetables can keep
us healthy.

carrot

Some vegetables grow under the ground.

peas

Some vegetables grow above
the ground.

Looking at Vegetables

onion

Some vegetables are short
and round.

bean

Some vegetables are long and thin.

Many vegetables are green.

beet

carrot

Some vegetables are orange
or purple.

How Vegetables Help Us

Vegetables are full of nutrients.

You need nutrients to stay healthy.

Eating carrots helps keep your skin and eyes healthy.

Eating spinach helps keep your blood healthy.

Eating sweet potatoes gives you energy.

You need energy to work and play.

Healthy Eating

Half of the foods you eat each day should be fruits or vegetables.

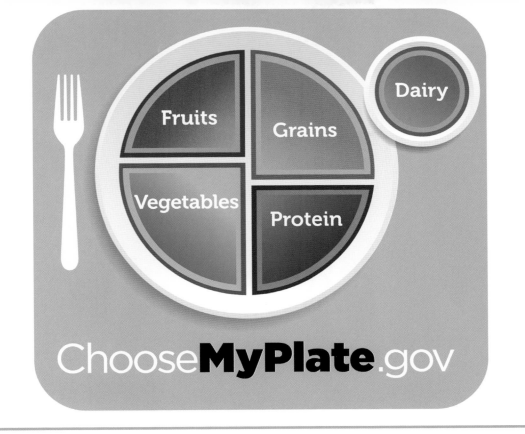

MyPlate reminds us to eat some foods from each food group every day.

We eat vegetables to stay healthy.

We eat vegetables because they taste good!

Find the Vegetables

Here is a healthy dinner. Can you find two vegetables?

Answer on page 24

Picture Glossary

blood red liquid inside your body. Blood takes food and air to all your body parts.

energy the power to do something. We need energy when we work or play.

nutrients things our bodies need to stay healthy. You can get nutrients in different foods.

Index

Answer to quiz on page 22: The two vegetables are carrots and broccoli.

Notes for parents and teachers

Before reading

Explain that we need to eat a range of different foods to stay healthy. Splitting foods into different groups can help us understand how much food we should eat from each group. Introduce the vegetables element on the MyPlate graphic on page 19. Draw children's attention to the fact that half of MyPlate is made up of fruits and vegetables. This means half of what they eat should be fruits and vegetables. Encourage children to eat a variety of vegetables every day.

After reading

- Choose children to mime some benefits of eating vegetables for the others to guess. These can include keeping our skin, teeth, and gums health, building strong muscles, healing cuts and bruises, fighting illnesses, helping us see in the dark, helping us to digest food and get rid of waste products.

- Create a bar chart or pictogram with the children to show the different vegetables they have eaten or tasted over the course of a week. Make it a challenge to see how high you can get the bar for each vegetable to go, and to see how many new vegetables can be added to the chart.

- Ask the children to bring in pictures of as many different vegetables as they can find. Divide the children into groups and ask the groups to explore different ways of sorting the vegetables. For example, they might sort them by shape, size, color, preference, or whether they can be eaten raw. Collages of grouped vegetables can be put up on the wall.